# Upon the Ch&#x2026;
# of the Ancient Cornish Language

*With some Observations about the Early Tin Trade*

## By Sherlock Holmes

## Truro: Bell and Brown 1898

*Edited and annotated by Kelvin I Jones,*

*With some additional observations regarding the toxicology of the 'Devils Foot'*

# INTRODUCTION

This slim and obscure volume on the Chaldean roots of the Cornish language was first discovered over 35 years ago by my old friend and savant, the antiquarian bookseller, John Ryder of Liskeard. It was discovered inside a copy of Sabine Baring – Gould's 'A Book of The West', he being the eminent Victorian historian and priest, himself a prolific author and collector of West Country curiosities.

The work was then passed on to me for further examination and possible verification.

Although I cannot be precise about the accuracy of its contents, there can be no doubt as to its scholarship and research. Sherlock Holmes, the world famous private consulting detective and criminologist, was well known as the author of a similarly obscure work on early English palimpsests and was also greatly admired for his magnum opus, 'The Art of Detection' which recently I had the good fortune to reissue.

Therefore, I am more than happy to attest to the diligence and remarkable observations contained in this short but curious work, despite the specious nature of some of its more dramatic and daring conclusions.

I have included with this volume some observations of my own, relating to Dr Watson's account of *the 'Adventure of the Devil's Foot'* regarding the possible toxicology of the drug which ruined the lives of the Cornish mining family and which required the analytical abilities of the Baker Street detective to provide a meaningful solution. For it was here on Cornwall's Lizard peninsula that Holmes first had the idea to conduct his researches into the roots of the Cornish language.

Kelvin I Jones

It has long been held that there are distinct resemblances between the Cornish language and the ancient Phoenician tongue. As I shall hope to demonstrate, this is not entirely provable but there is a measure of truth in the hypothesis. There is, however, a more than distinct possibility that the Phoenician civilization traded with the early inhabitants of this remote corner of our island.

The degree of their influence and commerce with the Cornish people can be ascertained from an examination of the Classical writers. From certain allusions or statements in old writers it has been assumed that in prehistoric times there was an export trade in British tin, shipped from an isle called Ictis, lying somewhere off the coast. This island, the story goes, became a peninsula at low water, and could then be reached by dry land, when the tin was brought to it and sold, shipped to Gaul and carried across to Marseilles on horseback.

Let us then proceed to establish that truth which has caused much doubt and wild guesswork without any satisfactory result. One should never guess, of course: it is destructive to the reasoning faculty.

Some authorities who have studied this subject believe that the island concerned should be St Michael's Mount, off Penzance; others, the Black Rock at Falmouth; others, St Nicholas's Island, at the mouth of the Tamar, near Plymouth; by others, the Isle of Portland; and by others, the Isle of Thanet, near Kent. Yet again, it has been asserted to be the Isle of Wight, solely because its name is somewhat like Vectis, the Latin name for that island. Sadly, archaeology and geography have been so ruthlessly violated on this vexed subject that so far, attempts to determine the question have ended in failure.

To substitute for the chaotic confusion and traditional fallacy, which have hitherto prevailed, a genuine, precise and critical examination of the story must be fairly acceptable and hopeful for the truth. It is an old dictum of mine that when you have eliminated the impossible, whatever, remains, however improbable, must be the truth.

Now we shall proceed to establish that truth. Pytheas, another writer of a later date, (c. BC 260), implies he came over to Kent and travelled in Britain, but he gives no hint about tin. There is now a gap of about two centuries. Then, in BC 50 (c.) one Posidonius is said to have crossed to Britain and to have given it the name Altiventeum, otherwise Bolerium. The name suggests an experience of the south west of Britain. He does not mention tin but tells us that beyond the Lusitanians (Portugal), in the Cassiterides, tin was found by digging for it. There is now a gap of some twenty years. Then, in B.C. 30, (approximately) we find Diodorus in Sicily writing about the inhabitants of Belerium:

"The inhabitants of Belerium are hospitable; and on account of their intercourse with strangers, more civilized and courteous in their habits than the rest are. These are people who make the tin, which they dig and melt and refine, and cast into ingots in the form of astragali, and carry it to an island near at hand called Iktis. At low tide, the land being dry between them and the island, they convey over in carts abundance of tin; hence the merchants transport the tin they buy of the inhabitants to Gaul, the opposite Continent, and then, by a thirty days' journey on horses' backs, to the mouth of the Rhone, to Marseilles and Narbonne, a great mart in those parts."

We now have a direct statement that tin was produced in Britain and that the place of production was Bolerium. Bolerium was, to the Romans, the extreme western edge of Britain, which we would describe as Cornwall. Diodorus goes on to say that "There is one thing peculiar to these islands which lie between Britain and Europe". These might well be the Scillies.

So far, we have merely speculation. Yet, the evidence would suggest that tin was being supplied to the ancient world for a long period of time, extending into the Bronze Age. If tin did come from Cornwall, as seems possible, is there any reason, therefore, why we should imagine there might be a link between the Cornish and the Phoenician languages?

From our study of the Hebrew writings, we may conclude that metallurgy was practiced very early. Tubal-Cain is said to have been "the instructor of every artificer in works of brass and iron." And we have only to consider the offerings of gold, silver and brass presented to Moses and the instruments and utensils, which the Israelites made for the tabernacle to realize that this art was well advanced in the ancient world. Pliny (lib. xxxiv. cap. xvii.) says that the art of tinning copper was also understood and practiced by the ancient Romans. The question remains whether tin used by the Ancients, and especially the Egyptians, was brought to them from the East or from the West.

That which Moses brought with him out of Egypt prove the likelihood of an extensive commerce with the East. The Rev Whitaker, in his learned *Treatise on the Commerce and Navigation of the Ancients, in the Indian Ocean*, says that "tin is mentioned as an import into Africa, Arabia, Scindi, and the coast of Malabar. It has continued an article of commerce brought out of Britain, in all ages, conveyed to all the countries in the

Mediterranean by the Phoenicians, Greeks, and Romans, and carried into the Eastern Ocean, from the origin of commerce."

It now becomes our duty to place before the reader the positive information which ancient authors have recorded respecting this traffic. By this means, he will be enabled to judge of the soundness of our conclusions, from data of acknowledged authority. These extracts will be given, as nearly as possible, in the order in which they were written, with an occasional observation when necessary.

Ezekiel, who prophesied about or soon after B.C. 600, in his brilliant catalogue of the traffic of Tyre, says," Tarshish was thy merchant by reason of the multitude of all kinds of riches: with silver, iron, tin, and lead, they traded in thy fairs." Ezekiel xxvii.

Herodotus, the well-known father of Grecian history, who wrote B.C. 440, says, with reference to this subject:-

*"Of that part of Europe nearest to the west, I am not able to speak with decision. I by no means*

*believe that the barbarians give the name of Eridanus to a river, which empties itself into the Northern Sea; whence, it is said, our amber comes. Neither am I better acquainted with the islands called the Cassiterides, from which we are said to have our tin. The name Eridanus is certainly not barbarous; it is of Greek derivation, and, as I should conceive, introduced by one of our poets. I have endeavoured, but without success, to meet with someone who, from ocular observation, might describe to me these which lies in that part of Europe. It is nevertheless certain that both our tin and our amber are brought from those extreme regions."*

Julius Caesar, about AD 40 made this statement.

"The inland parts of Britain are inhabited by those, whom fame reports to be the natives of the soil. The seacoast is peopled with the Belgians, drawn thither by the love of war and plunder. These last, passing over from different parts, and settling in the country, still retain the names of the several states whence they are descended. The island is well peopled, full of houses, built after the manner of the

Gauls, and abounds in cattle. They use brass money, and iron rings of a certain weight. The provinces remote from the sea produce tin; and those upon the coast, iron; but the latter in no great quantity. Their brass is all imported. All kinds of wood grow here the same as in Gaul, except the fir and beech-tree. They think it unlawful to feed upon hares, pullets, or geese; yet they breed them up for their diversion and pleasure. The climate is more temperate than in Gaul, and the cold less intense. The island is triangular, one of its sides facing Gaul. The extremity towards Kent, whence is the nearest passage to Gaul, lies eastward; the other stretches south-west. This side extends about five hundred miles. Another side looks toward Spain, westward. Over against this lies Ireland, an island esteemed not above half as large as Britain, and separated from it by an interval equal to that between Britain and Gaul. In this' interval lies the isle of Mona besides several other lesser islands, of which some write, that in the time of the winter solstice they have night for thirty days together. We could make out nothing of this upon inquiry; only discovered by means of our hourglasses, that the nights were shorter than in Gaul. The length of this side is computed at seven hundred miles. The last side faces the northeast, and is fronted by no part of the Continent, only towards one of its extremities; it seems to eye chiefly the German coast. It is thought to extend in length about eight hundred miles. The inhabitants of Kent, which lies wholly on the seacoast, are the most civilized of all the Britons, and differ but little in their manner from the Gauls. The greater part of those within the country never sow their lands, but live on flesh and milk, and go clad in skins. All the Britons in general paint themselves with woad, which gives a bluish cast to the skin, and makes them look dreadful in battle."

Diodorus the Sicilian wrote just before our era. He has given the following account of the Phoenician trade and the traffic with Britain for tin:

"The Phoenicians in ancient times undertook frequent voyages by sea, in the way of traffic as merchants, so that they planted many colonies both in Africa and in these western parts of Europe. These merchants, succeeding in their undertaking, and thereupon growing very rich, passed at length beyond the Pillars of Hercules, into the sea called the Ocean; and first they built a city called Gades, near to the Pillars of Hercules, at the sea-side, in an isthmus in Europe; in which, among other things proper for the place, they built a stately temple to Hercules, and instituted splendid sacrifices to be offered to him after the rites and customs of the Phoenicians. This temple is in great veneration at this day, as well as in former ages; so that many of the Romans, famous and renowned both for their births and glorious actions, have made their vows to this god, and, after success in their affairs, have faith- fully performed them. The Phoenicians, therefore, upon the account before related, having found out the coasts beyond the Pillars, and sailing along by the shore of Africa, were on a sudden driven by a furious storm afar off into the main ocean; and after they had lain under this violent tempest for many days, they at length arrived at this island ; and so coming to the nature and pleasantness of this isle, they were the first that discovered it to others.

"Over against the French shore, opposite to the

Hercynian Mountains, which are the greatest
of any in Europe, there lie in the ocean many
islands; the greatest of which is that which
they call Britain, which anciently remained
untouched, free from all foreign force; for it
was never known that either Bacchus,
Hercules, or any of the ancient heroes or
princes ever made any attempt upon it by
force of arms ; but Julius Caesar in our time
(who by his great achievements gained the title
of 'Divine') was the first that conquered the
island, and compelled the Britons to pay
tribute. But these things shall be more
particularly treated of in the proper time. We
shall now only say something concerning the
island, and the tin that is found here. In form,
it is triangular, like Sicily; but the sides are
unequal. It lies in an oblique line, over against
the continent of Europe; so that the
promontory called Qantium, next to the
continent, is, they say, about a hundred
furlongs from the land. Here the sea ebbs and
flows. But the other point, Balerium, is four
days' sail from the continent.

"The last, called Horcas, or Orcas, runs out far
into the sea. The least of the sides facing the

whole continent is seven thousand and five hundred furlongs in length; the second, stretching out itself all along from the sea to the highest point, is fifteen thousand furlongs; and the last is twenty thousand - so that the whole compass of the island is forty-two thousand five hundred furlongs. The inhabit- ants are the original people thereof, and live to this present time after their own ancient manner and custom. In fights, they use chariots, as it is said the old Grecian heroes did in the Trojan War.

"They dwell in mean cottages, covered for the most part with reeds or sticks. In reaping their corn, they cut off the ears from the stalk, and so house them up in repositories underground ; from thence they take them and pluck out the grains of as many of the oldest as may serve them for the day; and, after they have bruised the corn, make it into bread. They are of much sincerity and integrity, far from the craft and knavery of men among us, contented with plain and homely fare, strangers to the excess and luxury of rich men.

"The island is very populous, but of a cold climate, subject to frosts, being under' the

Arctic pole. They are governed by several kings and princes, who for the most part are at peace and amity with each other's. But of their laws, and other things peculiar to this island, we shall treat more particularly when we come to Caesar's expedition into Britain.

"Now we shall speak something concerning the tin that is dug and gotten there. They that inhabit the British promontory of Balerium, by reason of their converse with merchants, are more civilized and courteous to strangers than the rest are. These are the people that make the tin, which, with a, great deal of care and labour, they dig out of the ground; and that being rocky, the metal is mixed with some veins of earth, out of which they melt the metal, and then refine it; then they beat it into four square pieces like a die, and carry it to a British isle near at hand, called Ictis; for at low tide, all being dry between them and the island, they convey over in carts abundance of tin in the meantime."

Strabo, about A.D. 18, wrote on this subject: - "The Cassiterides are ten in number, and lie near each other in the ocean toward the north from the haven of the Artabri. One of them is desert, but the others are inhabited by men in black cloaks, clad in tunics reaching to the feet, girt about the breast, and walking with staves, thus resembling the furies we see in tragic representations. They subsist by their cattle, leading for the most part a wandering life. Of the metals, they have tin and lead, which, with skins, they barter with the merchants for earthenware, salt, and brazen vessels. Formerly, the Phoenicians alone carried on this traffic from Gades, concealing the passage from every one; and when the Romans followed a certain ship master, that they also might find the market, the ship-master of jealousy purposely ran his vessel upon a shoal, leading on those who followed him into the same destructive disaster ; he himself escaped by means of a fragment of the ship, and received from the state the value of the cargo he had lost. The Romans, nevertheless, by frequent efforts discovered the passage; and as soon as Publius Crassus, passing over to them, perceived that the metals were dug out at a little depth and that the men were peaceably disposed, he declared it to those who already wished to traffic in this sea for profit, although the passage was longer than that to Britain. Thus far concerning Iberia and the adjacent islands."

Pliny, who wrote about AD 79, has scattered throughout his "Natural History" several notices of Gades, tin, and the countries whence it is procured. He says, speaking of England, "Opposite to this coast is the island called Britannia, so celebrated in the records of Greece and of our own country;" then, having mentioned Hibernia, he says, "Of the remaining islands, none is said to have a greater circumference than one hundred and twenty-five miles. Among these there are the Orcades, forty in number, and situate within a short distance of each other, the seven islands called Acmodum, the Hebrides, thirty in number, and, between Hibernia and Britannia, the islands of Mona, Monapia, Rid.na, Vectis, Limnus, and Andros. Below it are the islands called Samnis and Axantos; and opposite, scattered in the German Sea, are those known as the Gimssarim but which the Greeks have more recently' called the Electrides, from the circumstance of their producing *electrum,* or amber.

"The most remote of all that we find mentioned is Thule, in which, as we have previously stated, there is no night at the summer solstice, when the sun is passing through the sign of Cancer ; while, on the other hand, at the winter solstice there is no day. Some writers are of opinion that this state of things lasts for six whole months together. Timmus, the historian, says, that an island called Mictis is within six days' sail of Britannia, in which white lead is found; and that the Britons sail over to it in boats of osier covered with sewed hides. There are writers, also, who make mention of some other islands; Scandia, namely, Dumna, Bergos, and, greater than all, Nerigos, from which persons embark for Thule. At one day's sail from Thule is the Frozen Ocean, which by some is called the Cronian Sea."

Writing of the "Islands in the Ocean," the same author says, " Opposite to Celtiberia are a number of islands, by the Greeks called Cassiterides, in consequence of their

abounding in tin; and, facing the promontory
of the Arrotrebae, are the six islands of the
gods, which some persons have called the
Fortunate Islands.     At     the     very
commencement of Betica, and twenty-five
miles from the mouths of the Straits of
Gades, is the island of Gadis, twelve miles
long and three broad, as Polybius states in
his writings. At its nearest part, it is less than
seven   hundred   feet   distant   from   the
mainland, while in  the remaining portion it
is distant more than seven miles. Its circuit
is fifteen miles, and it has on it a city which
enjoys the  rights  of  Roman  citizens,  and
whose people are called the Augustani of the
City of Julia Gaditana. On the side which
looks towards Spain, at about one hundred
paces' distance, is another long island, three
miles wide, on which the original city of
Gades stood. By Ephorus and Philistides it is
called Erythia,  by  Timaeus  and  Silenus
Aphrodisias, and by the natives the Isle    of
Juno.

"Timibus says, that the larger island used to
be  called  Cotinusa,  from  its  olives;  the
Romans call it Tartessos; the Carthaginians,

Gadir, that wording in the Punic language signifying ' a hedge.' It was called Erythia because the Tyrians, the original habitants and ancestors of the Carthaginians, were said to have come from the Erythraean or Red Sea. In this island Geryon is by some thought to have dwelt, whose herds were carried off by Hercules. Other persons, again, think that his island is another one, opposite to Lusitania, and that it was there formerly called by that name."

Further on in his treatise, when writing of lead mines and of white and black lead, Pliny says:

"The nature of lead comes next to be considered. There are two kinds of it, the white and the black. The white is the most valuable : it was called by the Greeks *cassitelos;* and there is a fabulous story told of their going in quest of it to the islands of the Atlantic, and of its being brought in barks made of osiers, and covered with hides. It is now known that it is the production of Lusitania and Gallaecia. It is a sand, found on the surface of the earth, and of a black colour, and is only to be detected by its weight. It is mingled with small pebbles, particularly in the dried beds of rivers. The miners wash this sand, and calcine the deposit in the furnace. It is also found in the gold mines that are known as *alutice,* the stream of water, which is passed through them detaching certain black pebbles, mottled with small white spots, and of the same weight as gold. Hence, it is that they remain with the gold in the baskets in which 'it is collected; and, being separated in the furnace, are then melted, and become converted into white lead.

"Black lead is not procured in Galhecia, although it is so greatly abundant in the neighbouring province of Cantabria; nor is silver procured from white lead, although it is from black. Pieces of black lead cannot be soldered without the intervention of white lead, nor can this be done without employing oil; nor can white lead, on the other hand, be united without the aid of black lead. White lead was held in estimation in the days even of the Trojan War - a fact that is attested by Homer, who calls it 'cassiteros.' There are two different sources of black lead : it being procured either from its own native ore, where it is produced without the intermixture of any other substance , or else from an ore which contains it in common with silver, the two metals being fused together. The metal which first becomes liquid in the furnace is called *stannum;* the next that melts is silver; and the metal that remains behind is galena, - the third constituent part of the mineral. On this last stage before being submitted to fusion, a black lead is produced, with a deduction of two-ninths."

"India has neither copper nor lead; but she procures them in exchange for precious stones and pearls. Black lead is used in the form of pipes and sheets. It is extracted with great labour in Spain, and throughout all the Gallic provinces; but in Britannia it is found in the upper stratum of the earth in such abundance, that a law has been spontaneously made, prohibiting any one from working more than a certain quantity of it."

# LAND OF THE ANCIENT GODDESS

Each year a long succession of pilgrims winds its way at low tide onto an island in Mount's Bay, near Marazion, in Cornwall. To say they are pilgrims is right: for, like many who visit a site of religious interest and power, they are drawn to this place for many reasons. Some are drawn here because of the history of the place; others because of the magical, almost fairy-tale atmosphere that prevails. In addition, for others there is a sense of indefinable power, which this island exudes. For the truth is that St Michael's Mount is a power centre which draws some people to itself like a magnet.

On the face of it, the Mount appears to be what

its historical record claims for it: a place of Christian antiquity. Yet, as we shall discover, its antiquity predates Christianity altogether and will lead us on a path of discovery which ends with the ancient deities of this remarkable land known by the Romans as "The Country of The Setting Sun."

Before we begin our quest into the historical record of the Mount, however, we might do well to embark on a physical pilgrimage. One thing that the casual observer may not appreciate is that the Mount has its fair share of shapes and faces in the rocks. As you approach the island along the path that leads past the dunes, keeping your back to the general direction of Penzance, stop by the ancient bridge, then follow the riverbank until the reach the point where the river casts itself into the sea. If you pause awhile, here you will immediately notice a sense of peace and calm. This is no illusion, no wishful thinking. It is a place where the spirit can be rejuvenated time and again. We should not be surprised at the experience. Our ancestors knew that such places were sacred. At the points where water gushed out of the earth, they paid homage by hanging clooties or rags to trees. They acknowledged the power of sites like these.

As one looks towards the island, one can see a face of a woman. Her face reclines against the rocks. It is undeniably the face of the Mother Goddess. Moreover, as you make your way across the broad sweep of the beach something remarkable becomes apparent: the face changes.

There are possibly three distinct faces and they are the faces of Maiden, Mother and Crone: the three aspects of the Goddess known by the ancients and celebrated in all ancient cultures, but especially the Celtic countries.

This revelation does not come suddenly to the viewer. At first, the faces are not clearly visible. It takes a detachment of the mind to encounter them. Yet they are undeniably there, standing on the face of the living rock, as if some giant sculptor had placed them there, aeons ago.

When this discovery was pointed out to me by a Cornish fisherman several years ago, it seemed strange at first that the Mount should be dedicated to St Michael. For what, I asked myself, was the connection between these ancient and unique faces with such an aggressively Christian symbol as St Michael?

The history and identity of this place of power cannot readily be appreciated without some understanding of the way in which the dominant religion of the land has "modified" and adapted the places held to be sacred by those who followed a very much older religion. To understand this, we must now go back in time to a period before the sixth century, even before the first Christian monks, those children of the Irish chieftain Brychan first set foot on this remote peninsula we now call Penwith.

Although our recorded history of the Mount takes us back only to the medieval period, there are many clues as to the true identity of the Mount as a place of worship of the Goddess. We know, of course, from our study of early religions that long before the rise of the patriarchal religions, Judaism, Christianity and Islam, people's perception of religion and spirituality derived from the belief in the all nurturing, all-powerful female deity who, to all intents and purposes was the very earth that people lived on. The earth was sacred to all early peoples as a close study of our surviving aboriginal people will demonstrate.

In Cornwall, as elsewhere in Britain, the population followed a belief in the divinity of the Goddess and she was, of course, known by many different names. Our modern archaeology has confirmed that local communities venerated this female deity in a number of different guises and in India today this is still true of the female aspects of the Goddess in the Hindu religion. When the Romans came to report on the identity of the deities worshipped by the Celtic people whom they successfully vanquished from Northern Europe, they naturally provided them with their own names, which became in turn the names of Roman gods and goddesses.

However, we can form some idea of the worship and the ceremonies, which were performed on the Mount at this remote date by examining what, prevailed in similar situations among people of the same origin on the coast of France.

Saint Michael's Mount in Normandy was called in the Roman period Mount Belen because it was dedicated to Belenus, described by the Roman historians as one of the four principal deities worshipped by the people they termed "the

Gauls" - a loose term for the Celtic people who inhabited France at the time. According to Roman historians on the French Mount was established a society of female Druids, the eldest of whom delivered oracles. These female Druids also furnished sailors with arrows, supposed to possess the virtue of appeasing storms when thrown into the sea by a young man of twenty-one years of age. On the return of the vessel safe to the port, the young man was then deputed to carry presents or offerings to these female Druids.

Another island, this one dedicated to Bacchus and described by Strabo as being on the Coast of Britain or Gaul, was famous for the oracle of a Gaulish deity. Here the priestesses, all virgins, were nine in number. They were called Gallicenae and were, according to Strabo, "supposed to possess great genius and rare endowments; capable of raising storms by their incantations; of transforming themselves into what animals they please; of curing diseases, reckoned by others incurable; quick at discerning, and able to foretell what is to come; but easy of access to sailors only, and to those who come to this island on purpose to consult them."

It is interesting to ponder on the attributes possessed by these women priestesses for they correspond exactly to the abilities Cornish witches were reputed to possess: divination, healing, the ability to raise storms, etc. It is also interesting to reflect that in both legend and fact women have possessed these qualities and been renowned for them in the far west of Cornwall.

The idea of a strong matriarchal community of Druids both in Northern France and here in West Cornwall among the Celtic societies of 2000 years ago is an intriguing one, yet it might not surprise us when we consider the enormously powerful influence Boadicea enjoyed in the eastern counties of Britain. Boadicea, like the priestesses of the Mount, could also shapeshift and had the power of divination to a remarkable degree. Such was her power that the revolt led by her almost destroyed Roman power in Britain. Could the far west of Britain therefore have enjoyed a druidical matriarchy on a similar level?

Although in Cornwall there are no Roman records to convince us of this, there is evidence. And although it is, by its very nature, fragmentary, it is there for us to observe. But before we do so, what exactly did the Roman writers mean by "druids"?

These sacred oak cultists were known in the ancient world by a number of different names. In Greek times, they were known as "dryads" or oracular priestesses whose souls dwelt in the trees. They could also assume the shape of serpents. In fact, dryadism and druidism were aspects of the same religion, a religion that was restricted to a female priesthood but which later became open to men. According to Lewis Spence, the occultist:

'There is no break between the ancient semi-magical formulae chanted by the Druids and the later incantation of the wizard and the "wise-woman". They both arose in the Veda-like sacred hymns, which formed the depository of the learning professed by the body of the druidical teachers and diviners and taught orally in the druidic schools. Most of them were never written down and the fragments that we possess in writing are probably only the remains of a considerable body of oral literature.'

The prominence of women in the druidic

tradition was attested to by numerous commentators in the ancient world and even after the advent of Christianity and the disappearance of pagan traditions in Northern Europe the female druidic tradition still clung to European consciousness. In Ireland, the priestesses of Brigit (or Bride to use her pagan name) lived in convent like sanctuaries and tended a sacred fire dedicated to the Goddess. In Christian times, the holy sisters were assimilated as nuns.

But enough of Druidic priestesses. What evidence is there that there was within Belerion (to use its ancient name) a cult of the Goddess? In fact, the evidence can be extrapolated from place names and artefacts.

The visitor to West Cornwall will hardly be unaware of the large number of Holy Wells, most of which are still venerated and kept beautiful by local inhabitants. At many of these wells, offerings are still made and clooties or strips of rags hung over bushes, which guard the wells for the purposes of healing. The earliest known commentator on well rituals in Cornwall appears to be Carew who wrote in the sixteenth century about Lady Nant's well, near Newquay:

"Little Colan hath less worth the observation; unless you will deride, or pity their simplicity, who sought at our Lady Nant's Well there, to foreknow what fortune should betide them, which was in this manner: upon Palm Sunday, these idle-headed seekers resorted thither, with a palm cross in one hand, and an offering in the other: the offering fell to the priest's share, the cross they threw into the well; which, if it swam, the party should outlive that year, if it sank, a short ensuing death was boded: and perhaps not altogether untruly, while a foolish conceit of this halsening might the sooner help it onwards."

This is interesting for here we have, clearly described an act of pagan worship and divination at what we might assume to be a Christian place of worship. Moreover, the Christian priest is here receiving the offerings made to the divinity of the well: proof positive that Christian clerics in Cornwall at this remote period had a foot in both religious camps: they served the Christian God and the ancient traditions with equal reverence! It is also interesting to see the cross itself, once a pagan symbol of fertility, being cast into the well as an offering. Now the well in question is called Our Lady Nant's Well.

The word Nant is identical with the pagan female deity Nanto-svelta, a water nymph in the northern European tradition. So here we have a pagan aspect of the Goddess being subsumed into the Christian tradition but being venerated by local people openly and with the support of their local parish priest.

An examination of the Feast Days in Cornwall also provides us with supportive evidence of the antiquity of the Great Mother and her widespread worship. A good example of this is Good Friday or, as the Cornish once called it, "Goody Friday". On this day (and the practice persisted until recent times, I am led to believe), according to Margaret Courtney, Cornish folklorist, "Every, vehicle was engaged days beforehand to take parties to some favourite place of resort in the neighbourhood, and labourers in inland parishes walked to the nearest seaport to gather "wrinkles"(winkles", etc.") Courtney also observes that "On the morning of Good Friday at St Constantine in West Cornwall, an old custom is still observed of going to the Helford River to gather shell-fish (limpets, cockles, etc.)"

Why limpet and winkle shells? What was the

object of this great pilgrimage? If one bothers to examine a limpet shell, one can see in an instant its strong resemblance to the female breast. Indeed, the Cornish word given by Lhuyd for limpet, "Brenigan", is itself a derivative of Bron, or "breast". One is reminded of that statue of Diana of Ephesus, the great and many-breasted goddess who represented to the ancient pagan world the Great Mother. So when we read of people going "a-trigging", picking up limpet shells on the edge of the tide (trig meaning the tide), we are seeing but a distant memory of the celebration of The Mother, occurring, of course, at the time of the great pagan festival of Eostre, which itself was a widely celebrated pagan festival long before it was adopted by Christians as a moveable, moon based feast.

In addition to the well ritual mentioned above, we also have the Holy Well at Madron, near Penzance. Here the evidence for veneration of a female deity is equally suggestive. The well has long been visited by local inhabitants during the month of May and at such times, it was customary, right up until very recent times, I am informed, for young women to resort to divination in an attempt to secure knowledge about their intended. Other customs included passing young children around the perimeter of the well in deosil fashion.

The name Madron is an intriguing one. The saints of Cornwall are, of course, notoriously unhistorical in their provenance and it is often the case that where a saint's name exists about whom there is very little information; we can assume that the name was imported from elsewhere and grafted onto an already existing pagan deity. This appears to be the case with Madron.

The earlier form of the name was "Madders" and its phonetic spelling may give us a clue as to its origin. There is an old Welsh deity called Modron who was indeed a Mother Goddess and it is most likely that here we have the case of a Saint, masking the true identity of an area perhaps once devoted to the Mother Goddess.

Madron itself was once regarded as the "Mother Church" and was important long before Penzance became significant. Inside the ancient 13th Century church, which bears the saint's name, there is a remarkable stone about six feet in height. The stone once lay hidden in the wall of the church but now stands adjacent to the belfry.

In the Madron church guide is what is inscribed as a "pagan phallic pillar" and this description does not err. On the face of the pillar is an inscription which recalls a now forgotten Celtic leader known as "the wolf". We know nothing further of him but may assume he was once the local tribal leader. More of interest, however, is a serpent, carved into the pillar, which rises up half its length. Serpents of this type are almost unheard of on British pillars of this period (dark ages) and would indicate some kind of fertility cult connected to goddess worship.

Most scholars believe that Penzance itself means "the holy headland" But why holy? We may assume that the "Holy Headland" was the rocky ridge which runs down from the market to the sea and which ends in a bluff before falling down to Battery Rocks. On this stands the church of St Mary The Virgin (St Mary, of course, has long been associated with Goddess worship throughout Christendom). A local tradition says that there was once a chapel of St Anthony, which was near Battery Rocks, but the Exeter records make no mention of any chapel of St Anthony at Penzance.

In some restoration work being conducted at the Barbican building in the late 1840's an ancient Celtic cross dating from the 6th century was discovered, and this may indicate the antiquity of the site. St Anthony was of course, the patron saint of fishermen - another link with the fishermen who were linked with the Druidical priestesses of the Mount. It is interesting that in the book called The High History of The Holy Grail, written in French in around 1200, it is said that King Arthur held high feast on St John's day after Pentecost in five separate years at "Pannenoisance which is situated on the sea of Wales."

Now the Grail history is one of the earliest mentions we have of Arthur and many scholars believe that the place mentioned is none other than Penzance for Cornwall was often referred to as West Wales. It is no coincidence that Arthur held his feast on St John's day for the Feast of St John has been celebrated here at Penzance for at least loo years and long after it had fallen into disuse elsewhere. The special bonfires that are lit on Midsummer's Eve (St John's Eve) have come down to us from the great Celtic tradition of the Summer Solstice and in Europe many of these celebrations still survive. But in Penzance they continued right up until the 1860s when they were effectively banned for their rowdiness.

Is the local Penzance festival of the Feast of St John a memory of that day when Arthur set foot on the Holy Headland? And, more importantly, why here? The headland itself, of course, faces St Michaels Mount. And herein lies the clue, which will, in turn, unlock the greatest of all mysteries.

Before leaving the question of the Midsummer Solstice celebrations, it would be well for us to remember that it was originally the Moon celebrations which were connected to the Midsummer sun celebrations of the shortest night and that this absorption must have been comparatively late for in some parts of France Midsummer Day itself is still called La Lunade, or "Moon Tide". Now there are a number of legends connected to ancient sites within the West Cornwall area also linked to the moon. One in particular is the legend of the Mermaid of Zennor, who lured one Matthew Trewella to his doom beneath the cliffs at Zennor. The sea sirens of the ancient world were, of course derived from the Greek sirens and connected to the Goddess

Aphrodite who herself shape-shifted in order to avoid the attentions of the sun god. She in turn was linked with the moon and is often depicted holding a sickle, which represents the crescent moon.

On the southern coast of the peninsula, meanwhile, we have the curious stone circle known as the Dans Maen (Merry Maidens). Legend has it that these were 19 maidens, turned to stone for dancing upon the Sabbath. Is this a far memory of a cult of priestesses who danced here to celebrate the moon's 19-year cycle round the earth?

The Harvest Moon is a time when the Moon is at its strongest and this occurs between September the 8th and October the 8th. The Cornish for Full Moon is Can and its anglicised form would be Cain. Is it possible, therefore, to find a Cornish Saint of dubious origin with that name? Curiously enough, we have St Keyne who turns out to be connected to none other than St Michael's Mount. What, then, do we know of St Keyne?

The old spelling of Keyne is, as Canon Doble points out, "Cain Breith, the daughter of

Brychan" and Brychan was an Irish Celtic chieftain whose daughters, it is believed, must have settled here sometime around the 6th Century. She had a famous holy well at St Keyne, near Liskeard, which was made famous in a ballad by the Victorian poet, Southey. In the ballad a stranger who visits the well is told that St Keyne once laid a spell on the well to the effect that if a husband drank first from its waters, he should be the master in the relationship but that if the wife drank first she would be the dominant partner. The legend is intriguing for it hints at a druidical priestess whose well gave power to women only if they made offering to the Goddess.

In John of Tynemouth's apocryphal life of St Keyne he claims that she was a "holy virgin" (it was common for Druid priestesses to be virgins in their service of the Goddess) and that she was visited at St Michael's Mount by Saint Cadocus whilst he was on a pilgrimage here. He notes that Cadocus implored her to leave but that "the people of the land would not permit it."

This is indeed a telling sentence for, if we assume that we are here dealing with a druidical holy virgin rather than what the medieval scribe might assume to be a Christian priest, it would make sense that she would be required to remain on the Mount as the guardian of the sacred site there.

Reverend Sable, in his account of the life of St Keyne, also mentions that at the top of the tower of the chapel on St Michael's Mount is "an ancient beacon, which has for centuries borne the name of "St Michael's chair." He quotes from Lyson's Magna Britannia (1814), who recalls that "the ascent to it is dangerous; but it is sometimes ascended out of a foolish conceit, that whoever sits therein, whether man or woman, will henceforth have the mastery in domestic affairs". And although Sable maintains that this tradition does not go back to before 1867, he offers no proof as to its real age. I rather suspect that this is a very old legend connected to the pre-Christian history of the island.

More interesting, perhaps, is the fact that St Keyne's Feast day is October the 8th, a possible date for the Harvest Moon. And, like the moon, we note, she is connected to love and matrimony, just like Aphrodite. Carew, in his very early history of Cornwall, notes that she is described as "no over-holy saint" which hints that she was perhaps celebrated with much licentiousness.

However, there is far stronger evidence than this that the Mount and its surrounding area were intimately connected to Goddess worship. In Chapter 26 of the medieval document Vita Cadoci, we read how St Cadoc visited "the Mount of St Michael, which is known to be in the region of the Cornishmen and in the idiom of that province is called Dinsol". Sable confuses the name with Denzel Downs, near Harlyn Bay, Padstow, but he is wrong to do so, for in the Welsh Book of Landaff, Saint Michael's Mount is also called Din Sul. What does this name signify for it is indeed the most ancient name we have for the Mount?

Before we begin to answer that question, we must take some time to look into the way the sun and the moon were regarded by the people of the Iron Age and even further back to the Neolithic period. First, it must be pointed out that throughout Northern Europe (where most of the inhabitants of these islands sprang from) the Sun was considered to be feminine in form. Thus in

Anglo-Saxon, "mona" - the moon - was a masculine word, and "sunne" - the sun - was feminine. The old and Middle Welsh word for the sun was "Haul" (feminine) and the moon was "Ileud" (masculine). In German, also, Die Sonne is feminine. If we consider the theory that at one stage in our evolution all priestly functions were the province of women, rather than men - and there is archaeological evidence to substantiate this view in the light of fairly recent discoveries - then it makes sense of the dedication of the Mount to Din Sul.

The name Din (or Dun) Sul can be easily translated. The word Din is a common word in the Celtic languages. It means simply a fortress. Sul is of course the old word for the Sun. However, there is much more to it than that, for Sulis was a Goddess whose dedications were widespread in the late Iron Age.

In the City of Bath, when excavation work was conducted as recently as 1875, a number of inscriptions were found in the Roman section of the baths to Deae Sulis, the Goddess Sulis. Caius Julius Solinus, a first century writer, informs us that at Bath Sulis was a British deity who "ruled over the boiling springs and at whose altar there flamed a perpetual fire which never whitened into ashes but hardened into a stony mass" - possibly an early reference to coal. Where have we met this "perpetual fire" before? Why in Ireland, where such a fire was dedicated to the Goddess Bride.

The dedication at Bath to Sulis was associated with her capacity of a healing Goddess. As Dr F. A. Ross points out in her Our Pagan Britain, "A divine couple, known from Gaul, Leucetius (equated with Mars) and nemetona (Goddess of the Sacred Grove) were also invoked at Aquae Sulis, situated as it was in a region in which traces of native faith abound."

One of the interesting finds at Bath was what has been described as a "male Medusa head". This serpent-wreathed symbol of protective power tended to be associated with healing springs. It was found on a pediment of the temple of Sulis. Although it is Roman in execution it is certainly Celtic in conception. It is interesting to reflect on the nature of the serpent as a symbol of female power and surely its appearance on the stone in Madron church is no coincidence.

Leucetius himself is an interesting deity. We know little more of him than that his name means "bright shining one" and that elsewhere he is depicted as the consort of the Goddess and that he was a horned god. The widespread worship of these deities is attested to by Dr Ross, who comments that:

"The temple at Bath was one of what would seem to have been a series of shrines associated with healing springs and their presiding deities, stretching right round the Severn Estuary to include the impressive temple at Lydney, and one at Caerwent. These are situated in an area in which traces of strongly defined local cults are plentiful, and it is clear that throughout the Roman period, cult legends of a rich and varied kind must have circulated about these native gods and goddesses and their classical counterparts."

From what we have discovered, we can say with certainty that Sul or Sulis was indeed a very ancient goddess who gave her name to the sacred site, which later came to be known as "St Michael's Mount." What then is the point of connection with St Michael?

The trail is easier to follow from this point onwards. St Michael is a saint who can be encountered on many of the hilltops of Cornwall and in other counties in Britain. In the Middle Ages St Michael became the focus for thousands of pilgrims who flocked to Saint Michel in Normandy and to St Michael's Mount in Cornwall because visions of the saint had been reported at these places. Legend has it that St Michael appeared to some fishermen who were sailing off Mount's Bay. The Christian archangel replaced the Goddess but retained her connection with both Sun worship and healing powers.

Places once used by Druids to invoke their own mercurial god of light became the focus for great pilgrimages, continuing a tradition that stretches back into prehistory.

It is no coincidence, surely, that of the eighteen parishes in West Cornwall, no less than twelve have feast or fairs on dates of sun worship. We know that the sun was indisputably worshipped on hill-tops and there is no doubt that St Michael was the successor to the sun goddess. Place names often give us clues. St Just in Penwith, one of the eighteen parishes mentioned above, has a stone circle known as Tregaseal. The old form of the name would have been Trega-seul - house of the sun.

Dr Borlase, who surveyed all of the ancient stone circles more than a hundred and fifty years ago, noted that the original number of the stones was 19 and that Boscawen-un, near St Buryan, still has nineteen to this day. It is perhaps significant that Apollo, the sun god, was reputed to have appeared to his followers every 19 years. And there are other correspondences. The Isles of Scilly, during the Romano-British period, had almost certainly become a shrine to the Goddess and on Nornour, now a deserted island; there is evidence of a shrine settlement. In one of the large huts excavated here, a large number of votive offerings were discovered including 300 brooches, coins, glass beads and clay figurines including Mother Goddess and Venus depictions.

The correspondence between the marine Goddess worshipped here, Sillina and the root word, sul or sil meaning "the eye" or "the light" is intriguing The word Suilli actually dates from c. AD 1200 and is therefore closer to the Celtic original of the word, "sul". And what of the curious name of Mousehole, which, on first examination, appears to make no sense. On closer examination we see that it is pronounced as "Mow-sel" which means "Sun (sul) place (mo, ma)" - place of the sun.

There is also evidence of the connection between sun and moon festivals if we are prepared to look far enough. In East Cornwall an important feast was celebrated on Hall Monday (prior to Shrove Tuesday) and on the evening of Hall Monday, according to Quiller Couch, children prowled the streets with short clubs, knocked on doors and took away with them anything worth stealing. The missing items were then displayed in incongruous places the following morning and, Quiller Couch notes, "The individuals concerned are supposed to represent some imps of darkness that seize on and expose unguarded moments." The date and time of "nicky Nan night" as it was called suggests a moon festival held at night. The moon is connected with fertility and the short clubs carried by the boys may represent phalli.

But what of Hall Monday? Hall is cognate with

heul, which in Cornish means "sun". And ball games, which in turn, are sun games, are still popular in parts of Cornwall at Shrove Tide. Hunt, writing in 1865, notes that "The game of "Hurling" was until a recent period, played in parishes to the west of Penzance on the Sunday afternoon" - a further indication of the link with the sun.

If we turn to East Cornwall, we have the curious stones known as the Hurlers. Were the Hurlers themselves a sun temple? Folklore tells us that the Hurlers were men turned into stone because they were wicked enough to play at Hurling on a Sunday. There is no doubt that Hurling was a sun game. In Brittany a similar game is entitled "Soulle" and there are correspondences in other Celtic countries, including Scotland.

The word "hurling" gives further proof of a Sun God or Goddess connection. There are a great number of dedications to "Ewe" contained in the Exeter Episcopal Registers and that the feast of St Ewe is on November 1st - the great Celtic fest day of Samhain or the beginning of the Celtic New Year. Hew (or Ewe) is a pronunciation in old Welsh of the name Hu.:

Hu (Hu-as, Hu-an), often known as Hu gadarn, "Hu the Mighty", was a great sun-god. Taliesin tells us that his chariot (and most sun-gods had chariots) was "an atom of glowing heat". Another Welsh poet sings: "And now the lofty leader, Huan, is about to ascend: the sovereign most glorious, the Lord of The British Isle." Like most sun gods, Hu was at first a culture deity. The Welsh Triads narrate that he taught his people "the way to plough when they were in the Summer Country before they came to Britain. The location of the Summer Country is a standing puzzle. But insomuch as Hu was the name of an Egyptian sun-god, we may venture to surmise that the "Summer Country" was Egypt. Hu was one of the sun gods attendants upon Ra, the greatest of sun-gods. Hu is also the Egyptian name of the Great Sphinx at Gaza, and this connection Sir Wallis Budge observes: "The men who made the Sphinx believed they were providing a colossal abode for the spirit of the sun-god which they expected to dwell therein and to protect their dead: it faced the rising sun, of which it was a mighty symbol."

There is a further correspondence between Hu and the Cornish landscape. Launceston had a

Midsummer Day fair and the old name for Launceston is Dunheved. Norden writes this name Dun-heu-ed in 1498. Ed is a place so Dunheved may well mean "Hill of Hu". He goes on to conjecture that Hu may have been the rising sun while Sul was the setting sun. What we may have here is a male and female aspect of the deities, both worshipped and venerated at particular points of the landscape and at particular times of the year, incorporating the rotation of the seasons.

If indeed St Michael's Mount was at the centre of a great pagan vortex of ceremonial sun and moon worship, which persisted until the early Dark Ages, is there any evidence that its reputation persisted into the middle Ages? Well, apart, from its popularity among pilgrims, there is other evidence.

One of the oldest accounts we have of the Mount comes from the pen of William of Worcester whose itinerary, compiled in the year 1478, deserves our attention. It is, properly speaking, a notebook containing a great deal of topographical comment. In the itinerary he inserts a papal indulgence addressed to "the church of Mount St

Michael in Tumba in the County of Cornwall". This term tumba is interesting for its meaning is the same as the English "tump", meaning a burial mound or sacred site. William next mentions the apparition of St Michael in Mount Tumba, formerly called the "Hore-rock in the Wood", which happened at a time when the woodland and meadow and plough land lay between the said Mount and the islands of Scilly and he recalls that there were "240 parishes now submerged."

The first apparition of St Michael in Mount Gorgon in the Kingdom of Apulia took place in AD 391; the second at Tumba in Cornwall, near the sea, about 710 AD; the third in the days of Pope Gregory at a time of "great pestilence"; and the fourth being "in ierarchiis nostrorum angelorum". The next paragraph appears to be the fragment of a description of Mont St Michel in Normandy and its foundation by St Aubert, bishop of Avranches.

When William visited the Mount, the priory was in possession of Augustinian nuns known as Bridgettines but of them, William says absolutely nothing. Not only, then, do we have a company of women in charge of the priory at this comparatively late period but they are also dedicated to Bridget whose sacred flame was-kept alive in Ireland until so late in the Middle Ages. Bridget, the reader hardly needs to be reminded, is but a Christianized form of the Goddess Bride who herself was connected to fire making, smith craft and poesy - all of them Druidical pursuits! The Bridgettine nunnery lasted here until 1536 when it was suppressed, like many monasteries in the period of the Reformation.

We now know, then, that St Michael's Mount was from earliest times a place of worship to The Goddess and that the whole of the area anciently known as Belerion was devoted to a form of Sun worship. There appears also to have been a strong tradition of Druidical priestesses who had established a community on the island from early times and that their power and influence was widespread, stretching possibly to the Isles of Scilly. At certain times of the year, but especially at the Solstices, the tradition of lighting fires upon the hill tops was established, a tradition that continued among the Cornish people for centuries and which is still maintained now. But what of St Michael and the Christianization of the island?

We know that devotion to the Archangel dates back to Jewish times and that it appeared very early among Christians. If we are to believe Simeon Metaphrastus, a Greek hagiographer of the tenth century, the first apparition of St Michael took place in Phrygia at the end of the first century. Sozomen and Nicephorus also describe an apparition of St Michael to the Emperor Constantine in the early part of his reign, which was in turn commemorated by the building of a church at Constantinople. In fact, a shrine to the honour of St Michael was found in the neighbourhood of Constantinople on the site of a former temple dedicated to Esculapius, the healing god.

This devotion to the Archangel soon spread from the East to the West, the first manifestations being found in Southern Italy and culminating, as we have seen at the sanctuary of Monet Gargano where St Michael appeared on 8 May, 492. This shrine became one of the great centres of medieval pilgrimage and so 8 May became St Michael's feast day. It is certainly significant that

St Michael's feast day subsequently became the day for the famous Helston Flora Day and that St Michael is still depicted slaying the dragon in the Hal an Tow ceremony which forms the oldest part of the celebrations. It is certain that the old Furry Dance once took place on 1st May, Beltane in the Celtic calendar but that, probably sometime in the Middle Ages, the date got changed.

For five centuries, then, the two Mounts - the one in Normandy and the one in Cornwall - stood as sentries on the Northern and Southern coasts of the English Channel. The French Saint Michel was the Mother House and the Cornish one the Daughter house. But both were visited by crowds of eager pilgrims. The road through Cornwall led first to Bodmin where the relics of St Petroc could be seen. Pilgrims came from far away - even from the continent, for we have records of French Canons arriving at Bodmin from Laon in 1133.

The reputation of the Mount as a place of healing - which it had always been, even in the days of the Goddess, who still presides here, under the great building which dominates its top -was confirmed, when I chanced upon a handwritten annotation in a margin of an ancient manuscript which he had been permitted to study at the great library in Avranches. I duly translated it and published the account. The miracles that were recorded happened, it seems, in the late 13th century and it is surely significant that the people who received healing here were ALMOST ALL WOMEN. The manuscript is worth quoting in its entirety:

"MS. No. 159 is the most valuable book in the Public Library of Avranches, which contains what remains of the library of the Abbey of Mont St Michel. It appear to be the original chronicle which Abbot Robert of Torigni presented to Henry 11 in 1184, and which he afterwards completed, bringing it down to the time of his death in 1186. The Chronicle is preceded by three pages containing miscellaneous matter written much later, as follows: first, a story of a miraculous flame on Mont St Michel in 1270; next, a list of books given to the Abbey of Bec by Philip, Bishop of Bayeux, in the time of Robert of Torigny. Then, on the lower half of the second column of folio 3, which must originally have been left blank, has been squeezed in, by a later hand, the following passage:

"Let no one going to the Monastery of St Michael in Cornwall doubt that a certain woman, named Christina, of the neighbourhood of Glastonbury, who had been deprived of the sight of her eyes for about six years, coming with the greatest devotion to the said monastery for the sake of prayer and pilgrimage, on 14th of May, 1262, before high Mass, on a certain Sunday, in the sight of the people, persevering in the greatest faith, by the intercession of the Blessed Archangel Michael, recovered miraculously (lit., divinely) the sight of her closed eyes. There were present as witnesses many monks and others, in the same year, on the 11th of June, a certain woman named Matilda, of the parish of Lanescli (Gulval), who for two days and two nights had lost consciousness and the power of speech, being brought by her parents to that monastery, on Sunday, immediately she had entered the church, by the prayers of the Captain of the Heavenly Chivalry, was restored to consciousness and power of speech. I saw it and was present. The Prior of that place then was Ralph Viel. In the same year a certain girl named Alice, of the parts of Hereford, born in Wales, who for seven years past had been deprived of the sight of her eyes, coming with the greatest devotion to the said church for the sake of prayer and pilgrimage on the 29th of January, before the rising of the sun, on a certain Monday, persevering in the greatest faith, by the prayers of the Blessed Archangel Michael recovered miraculously the sight of her closed eyes. The socii of that place then were Peter De Vallibus, Engelran of Bayeux, Maurice Taboeier, when those miracles happened in that church. The fourth miracle, on a certain dumb man, is in the beginning of this book on page 7, in the year of Our Lord, 1262, on the 2oth of August."

The reader is left feeling as if he could read more about these remarkable events but all we get is a chink in the curtain of history. It would appear that the writer does not give his identity and he may well have been a monk deputed to keep a register of healings and miracles by the Prior of St Michael's Mount. But whatever the case, we can be certain that these were not the only acts of healing which had taken place in the 13th Century at the Mount.

One notable detail is that the woman referred to

as Alice from Hereford was cured as the sun rose, its rays presumably piercing the light of the chapel window. Or was Alice outside on the Mount, facing east and praying? We can picture this for ourselves and imagine those ancient heads of the Maiden, the Mother and The Crone. Was Alice aware, one wonders, of the island's antiquity upon which she no doubt stood? Hundreds of years had elapsed between the time when this island was a place of the prophetesses and priestesses and the dawning of the age of Christendom, yet the place itself had not changed and neither has it since the Middle Ages.

Din Sul, as I prefer to call this sacred place, has retained in its outward form and in its spiritual power the arcane but vibrant strength of the landscape. And that is why so many pilgrims, even back in the early nineteenth century, flocked to see this magical island rising out of the waters of Mount's bay.

In his Ecclesiastical History of the English people, the venerable Bede, who died in 735 and who wrote the most famous of all of the accounts of the Dark Ages, quotes a letter written by pope

Gregory in 601 to an Abbot named Mellitus who was at that time on a missionary visit to these islands. The content of this letter, both wise in its understanding of the power of paganism and in its tolerance for the validity of other faiths, reminds us of how, even after nearly two thousand years, the great sanctuary of Din Sul, or the Hill of the Mother Goddess, remains defiantly unchanged:

"With regard to the case of the English, I have, after mature deliberation, decided as follows: that the temples of the idols of that nation ought not to be destroyed, but the idols themselves that are in them should be destroyed, and holy water must be made and sprinkled in those temples; also altars must be erected and relics deposited therein. For if the temples are well built, they must be converted from the worship of devils to the service of the true God; that the people... may remove error from their hearts... and may ..., resort habitually to the places to which they have been accustomed. And because they have been used to slaughter many oxen as sacrifices to devils, some religious observance must ... be substituted for these sacrifices, so than on the day of the dedication (of their church), or (on the occasion) of the feast days of the holy martyrs whose relics are deposited (in the church), they may build themselves huts of the boughs of trees around those churches which have been converted from (pagan) temples. Thus they may celebrate the solemn day with religious feasting, and no more offer beasts to the Devil, but kill and eat cattle to the praise of God, and return thanks to the Giver of all things for what they eat, so that while some of their (former) festivities are outwardly preserved, they may more easily agree to accept the inner joys (of the grace of God.) For there is no doubt that it is possible to efface everything at once from obstinate minds, for he who endeavours to ascend to the higher place, rises by degrees or steps and not by leaps."

That last sentence rings in our minds and reminds us that, even today, when spirituality is sometimes in question, we find fascination among many people that such sites can act as dynamos of power. To stand and face the Mount is to experience still that great feeling of peace and healing which floods like a beacon of light from the island once called Din Sul.

In this short work I have endeavoured to understand something of its strange and circuitous history. But to understand with the head is one thing; it is quite another to understand with the heart. The ancient deities of the land once called Belerion, or as the Romans termed it, "The Country of The Setting Sun."

Is there any evidence of the identity of the Goddess so fervently revered in this area of west Cornwall? And can we show examples of a continuing tradition of that worship in the folklore of that area?

Interestingly, Cornwall, more than any other area of Britain, perhaps, has a tradition of fairs and festivals connected to what in former times would have been localised deities.

One such feast is the fair held annually at the town of Liskeard which now is held on the 2nd of October but which in former times was held on the autumn equinox, which is September 21st. In the Doomsday book we find the old spelling of Liskeard is Lis-carret, which, being translated means "Caret's Enclosure".

The old goddess known by the name of Caridwen is mentioned many times in books of local folklore and in the Welsh Book of Taliesin her court is referred to as Yn Llys Caridwen, "in the Court of Caridwen." The "wen" of Caridwen may mean "white, pure or holy", which means that Lys Carid would approximate to Lis - caret. If I am right, then it would certainly make sense of a number of traditions which have survived into the 19th century.

The Welsh goddess Kerid or Carid was renowned for her acts of transformation and in Cornwall there are many tales of witches transforming themselves into hares - yet another symbol of the Goddess. Taliesin, in his telling of the tale of Cerridwen, puts these words into his own mouth: "I have been a grain... I was received by the hen with red fangs and a divided comb". This is an indication that Cerridwen was a fertility goddess, for elsewhere Taliesin remarks: "I have been for the space of nine months in the womb of Kerridwen The Fury..." So Keridwen was a fertility goddess, a hen, a moon goddess and a hare.

In the ancient ceremony of the Crying of the Neck, still performed in Helston, we have a fertility ritual in Cornwall which is a living testimony to the endurance of the Corn Goddess. Here, the last sheaf of wheat is cut by a sickle and held on high and the word "I have ee, I have ee, I have ee " are uttered, to which the reply goes up: "What ave ee, etc," then "A neck ! "

The neck of wheat is now taken into a local church and kept there all winter but in former days it was put over a fireplace. The point of this ritual is that we are seeing the spirit of the corn goddess being revered. The sheaf is kept as a way of honouring the Goddess and the land and to ensure a good harvest the following year.

In Altarnun Church there is a bench end on which the visitor may see the Corn Goddess well illustrated. Her skirt is made from corn and she resembles strongly some of the ancient figurines discovered in the east of Europe at places of Goddess worship. Dr Borlase reported a discovery of two hoards of gold coins found on Cam Brea, near Cambome in 1749. On one side of the coins is the face of a woman with long flowing hair and on the other is a horse. Sir John Rhys Evans believes these to be about 200 to 150 BC but they may be later. The coins are interesting because of the strength of the designs.

Clearly this is no ordinary woman we are looking at, nor is it a Roman empress. Could it be A Romano-British leader? I think that would be unlikely. My own view is that we are looking at a very early representation of the Goddess of fertility, whether she was called Cerridwen, Kerid, or whatever. Equally fascinating is the horse on the obverse side. There are two horses, each slightly different of the other. One of the horses has four teats which are exuding milk. But the horse has a beak, and not a mouth. What we are most reminded of when we look at the horses is the White Horse of Uffington. Is it - possible that we have here a symbolic representation of Epona, the great Celtic horse Goddess?

Epona was not envisaged as being herself equine but the horse was her totem animal. In fact in Britain we have a huge number of depictions of Epona and she was adopted by many Roman cavalry units stationed in Celtic areas like Cornwall. She is often portrayed lying half naked on a mare's back and she had the honour of being the only Celtic deity to be revered in Rome itself. Epona was herself born of a mare, for the Greek writer Agesilaos tells us that "(The mare) gave birth to a beautiful little girl whom she named

Epona."

She was, of course, a great goddess of fertility and is often shown carrying a SHEAF OF CORN, a cornucopia or a goblet or holding a SERPENT.

There is other evidence of Epona being worshipped in Cornwall. The church with the strange name of St Michael Penkevil (not far from Truro), for example, appears in the records of 1290 to be named Penkevel and Pen Kevel means "the horse's head".

Later, of course, St Michael comes on the scene and the name is added in order to Christianize the Goddess. In the Feast of St John, a curious dance can be seen making its way through the streets of Penzance which incorporates a horse's skeletal head held on a pole, accompanied by a teazer who is Bucca, a water deity. This is not a modem invention, though, for when the Spaniards sacked Paul church, near Newlyn, they found a horse's head which was kept in the church just for such an occasion.

But perhaps the finest of all survivals exists at Padstow, where, on each May 1st, a strange dragon-like creature is brought out from the back of a pub and then dances through the streets of this ancient town accompanied by hypnotic drumming.

This ritual is so ancient that no one really knows whence it originated. An examination of the figure itself gives us clues, for the creature has a beak and is known, of course as the "Oss." It is interesting, this word "Oss", for although on the one hand it can be thought of as a corruption of Horse, on the other hand there is an old English word, "Os" which literally means a deity. One of the legends about the Padstow Oss is that if a woman is caught under its skirts, she is immediately made pregnant.

So we have here a symbol of fertility - and a very potent one. (An old phrase, "to horse with a man" meant to have sexual intercourse). At times, throughout the long day the Oss falls down but is then revived by the singing of the crowd, an indication that the fertile energy of the Goddess can be renewed if the correct rituals are performed. The Oss of Padstow, then, is the clearest link we have with the ancient goddess venerated at Din Sul centuries ago.

In this short and admittedly, conjectural account

of classical records regarding the ancient history of Cornwall and its links to the Phoenicians, I have only touched the surface of the question as to whether Cornish as we know it today was derived in some part from the language of the Chaldees. This must, perforce, be devoted to a future and more comprehensive study. There is at present no direct *empirical* evidence to prove to me that it was. There remain, however, *indications* that the history of these remote places, steeped as they were in ancient beliefs and folklore, stories of ancient traders, the currency of tin and legends of pagan, goddess worshipping cults, is a great deal more complex and more fascinating, than most scholars, both past and present, would have us believe.


Sherlock Holmes

# DEVIL'S FOOT ROOT

*"It has not found its way either into the pharmacopoeia or into the literature of toxicology. The root is shaped like foot, half-human, half goat-like, hence the fanciful name given by a botanical missionary. It is used as an ordeal poison by the medicine men in certain districts of West Africa, and it is kept as a secret among them. This particular specimen I obtained under very extraordinary circumstances in the Ubanghi country."*

-Dr Leon Sterndale, DEVI.

It was in the spring of 1897[1] when Sherlock Holmes came face to face with one of the most bizarre cases of poisoning which he was ever to

---

[1] Dr Watson, DEVI

confront in his long and distinguished career. It will be recalled that, having suffered a breakdown,[2] he and Watson travelled to the remote Cornish village of Tredannack Wollas, near Poldhu Bay. It was here that the obscure and deadly "Devil's Foot" killed two people and drove two others to insanity.[3]

This poison had been taken from the possessions of Dr Leon Sterndale, the explorer, to enable Mortimer to destroy his sister Brenda Tregennis. As Dr Sterndale relates, the drug was kept among his African mementoes, for he had obtained it whilst on an expedition in West Africa.

"One day, only a couple of weeks ago, he came down to my cottage and I showed him some of my African curiosities. Among other things I exhibited this powder, and I told him of its strange properties, how it stimulates those brain centres which control the emotion of fear, and how either madness or death is the fate of the unhappy native who is subjected to the ordeal by the priest of his tribe. I told him also how powerless European science would be to detect

---

[2] Holmes suffered from manic depression.

[3] Brenda and Mortimer Tregennis died: Owen and George went mad.

it. How he took it I cannot say, for I never left the room, but there is no doubt that it was then, while I was opening cabinets and stooping to boxes, that he managed to abstract some of the devil's foot root."

What precisely was this poison which brought death and vengeance to a quiet corner of Cornwall? Certainly, it has not been officially listed in the pharmacopoeia under the name given it by Dr Sterndale, so we must look elsewhere for its source and identity. But before doing so, let us consider the evidence made available to us by Dr Watson.

According to Dr Sterndale, the poison otherwise called radix pedis diaboli) was virtually unknown among Western toxicologists. '... save for one sample in a laboratory in Buda,[4] there is no other specimen in Europe. It has not yet found its way into the pharmacopoeia or into the literature of toxicology. The root is shaped like a foot, half human, half goat like; hence the fanciful name given by a botanical missionary."

Dr Sterndale did not possess the poison in its

---

[4] Buda - Pesth or Budapest, capital of Hungary.

original state, but produced what is described in the narrative as "a reddish-brown powder" which he claimed to have obtained "in the Ubanghi country."[5] of Western Africa.

The effects of this psycho-active drug are recorded by Dr Watson in that remarkable experiment carried out by Holmes in the Cornish cottage:

"I hardly settled in my chair before I was conscious of a thick, musky odour, subtle and nauseous. At the very first whiff of it my brain and my imagination were beyond all control. A thick, black cloud swirled before my eyes, and my mind told me that in this cloud, unseen as yet, but about to spring out upon my appalled senses, lurked all that was vaguely horrible, all that was monstrous and inconceivably wicked in the universe. Vague shapes swirled and swam amid the dark cloud-bank, each a menace and a warning of something coming, the advent of

---

[5] Part of French equatorial Africa. This eastern colony, lying North of the Belgian Congo and East of Sudan, derives its names from two rivers, the Ubangi and the Shari, which flow into the Chad. Although cotton is the chief export, the area was until recently, virtually untapped. It covers an area of 238, 767 square miles.

some unspeakable dweller upon the threshold,[6] whose very shadow would blast my soul. A freezing horror took possession of me. I felt that my hair was rising, that my eyes were protruding, that my mouth was opened, and my tongue like leather. The turmoil within my brain was such that something must surely snap. I tried to scream, and was vaguely aware of some hoarse croak which was my own voice, but distant and detached from myself."

The fear-inducing properties of the drug are graphically conveyed in this passage which admittedly has a great deal of literary embellishment but nevertheless conveys the essential claustrophobia of the original experience.

Clearly the term "Devil's Foot" is a convenient one, probably employed by Dr Watson because he did not wish to publicise the remarkable ability of the poison to leave no trace in the body of the deceased. Peter Cooper[7] observes that "the

---

[6] A phrase H.P. Lovecraft, the American fantasist, was to adapt as a title of one of his supernatural collections.

[7] "The Devil's Foot - An Excursion into Holmesian Toxicology", pp. 59 - 61.

same title is given by the Apaches and Comanches to the peyote or mescal button; but peyote is euphoriant and produces brightness rather than blackness of vision and mood. Moreover, its provenance and setting are hopelessly at fault."

There are, however, a number of points which should lead us to the identification of radix pedis diaboli.

1. It comes from West Africa, NOT the South American continent.

2. It is pure, organic-derived poison. (Dr B. Koelle[8], has suggested lysergic acid, but the formula of this drug was not invented until 1943 in a Swiss laboratory.)

3. It is shaped like a foot and when ground up assumes a reddish-brown colour.

4. It also has a Latin name. As Verner Andersen points out[9], "Such names are usually only given to vegetable drugs when they are standardised by

---

[8] "Leaves From the Copper Beeches", 1958. Dr Koelle was head of the toxicological department of the well-known Swiss pharmaceutical firm of Sandoz.
[9] Radix Pedis Diabolis, SHJ, Winter 1975, pp. 54 - 55

a description in a pharmacopoeia or a similar formulary." In other words, the poison had already

been classified by western toxicologists.

5, It is a psycho-active drug, used as an ordeal poison. These drugs have been thoroughly investigated by western observers and by the 1890's considerable documentation had been made of their varieties. In fact, as Andersen demonstrates,[10] the only drug mentioned in the British Pharmacopoeia of 1885 (the volume which would have been available to Dr Watson) that originates from the Ubanghi area of West Africa is the dried seed of the Physostigma Venenosum, otherwise known as the Calabar Bean.

However, before any concrete decision is made about the Calabar Bean, let us examine the other possible contenders.

The first of these is Datura stramonium, offered to us as a possibility by Peter Cooper,[11] (otherwise known as L'Herbe au Diable, or thorn

---

[10] *ibid*
[11] *ibid* (n7) [2]

apple.) This plant contains active principles similar to those found in atropa belladonna (deadly nightshade.). The active principal constituents are atropine and hyoscine. Datura has a distinguished history and was purported to have been employed by the Delphic oracle.[12]

Datura Stramonium was also used extensively in the Middle Ages by Italian poisoners who developed a brew, which instantly deadened the senses of the victim. In India it was rumoured that Hindu prostitutes gave their clients Datura so as to render them unconscious for long periods of time. Considering the nature of their occupation, this seems a very practical method of dampening male ardour.

During the late 18th Century white slave traders administered a concoction of aphrodisiacs and Datura to their victim. When they awoke, their virginity and all memory of their experience had disappeared.

Datura contains three active alkaloids: atropine,

---

[12] *The Priestess of the God (called the Pythia) sat on a tripod over a crack in the rock and uttered words in her divine trance. These were then interpreted by another in the form of verses.*

scopolamine and hyoscyamine. Both atropine and scopolamine are extremely dangerous drugs, so much so that their dosage is recommended only between 1/500 and 1/100 of a grain. And both have a direct effect on the central nervous systems, causing a disruption in mental association. As one early writer described its effects:

"He who partakes of it is deprived of his reason; for a long time laughing or weeping, or sleeping and often times talking and replying, so that at times he appears to be in his right mind, but really being out of it and not knowing to whom he is speaking, nor remembering what has happened after his alienation has passed."

The one factor which casts doubt upon the identification of Datura as the Devil's Foot is that it induces vomiting when administered orally, as Peter Cooper correctly observes, [13] and it is unlikely that it would have the effects observed by Holmes and Watson when absorbed through the lungs.

Peter Cooper suggests the ordeal drug known as

---

[13] *ibid* (n7) [2]

muavi (Erythrpleum guineense) which was popular among witch doctors in the Congo region. His main reason for this suggestion appears to be that Doyle himself travelled to West Africa in 1881 where he "penetrated above Old Calabar into the mangrove swamps."[14]

Another claim has been made by F.A. Allen[15] who prefers reserpine in the shape of Rauwolfia vomitoria. This is a shrub that grew in abundance in the Belgian Congo at one time but it was of such a height (eighteen feet) that harvesting it became uneconomic. The relatives of rauwolfia vomitoria (rauwolfia serpentina, rauwolfia tetraphylla, etc.) have provided the main source of reserpine which is now produced synthetically as a sedative and tranquillizer.[16] It seems unlikely that this drug provided the source of the Devil's Foot since, like Datura, it is usually administered orally and causes severe vomiting.

Another contender is hemp. Since this drug is smoked like tobacco, it is a distinct possibility.

---

[14]Doctor Varro E. Tyler, Professor of Pharmacology at Purdue University, Indiana, disagrees. He prefers niando, also used by the Congo natives, mainly as an intoxicant. See SHJ, Vol 8, No. 2, p.61.
[15] M & B Pharmaceutical Bulletin 5, 1956, p. 118.
[16]Rauwolfia as a genus of plants was named by Charles Plumier in 1703. It comprises over eighty varieties of plant.

As Peter Cooper observes, Du Chaillu, the explorer, noted hemp smoking among the Ashira and Apingi of the Congo as long ago as 1861. "Practised smokers are soon laughing, talking, quarrelling and acting in all respects like drunken persons. Insanity is often its ultimate result on those who persist in its use."

Hemp is of course a psycho-active drug, and an extremely vivid account of its effects on the user was made by Theophile Gautier in 1843[17] He records:

"After several minutes a sense of numbness overwhelmed me. It seemed that my body had dissolved and become transparent. I saw very clearly inside me the hashish I had eaten in the form of an emerald which radiated millions of tiny sparks... All around me I heard the shattering and crumbling of jewels of all colours; songs renewed themselves without ceasing as in the play of a kaleidoscope. At certain moments I still saw my comrades, but disfigured and grotesque, half men, half plants."

It is interesting to note that at first the user

---

[17]Le Club des Hachichins.

experiences disembodiment. Then both his sight and hearing are affected and distorted. As Harold Burn remarks,[18] there is a close link between the effects of hashish and those of mescaline.

Let us now return to the Calabar Bean, otherwise known as Physostigmatis Semen, the dried seed of Physostigma Venenosum.

The plant was first discovered by the Reverend W.C. Thompson who in 1859 sent some flowering specimens to Professor J. H. Balfour of Edinburgh.[19] It was Balfour who in 1860 gave the plant its Latin name, but it was Robert Christison who first demonstrated its toxic effects.[20]

The Physostigma venenosum contains an active ingredient known as physistigmine. It is used mainly as a treatment for glaucoma and reduces the pressure experienced inside the eyeball. Among the chiefs of the Calabar region, however, the plant was considered to be sacred and it was closely guarded until the time of the

---

[18] "Drugs, Medicines And Man", p. 209
[19] See Verner Andersen's Radix Pedis Diabolis, SHJ, Winter 1975, p.55.
[20] Reprinted in "Two Hundred Years of Materia Medica at Edinburgh, 1968."

rituals. Several hundred people were killed each year during the rituals which were attended by the King and his principal courtiers. The victims, most of whom were convicted of witchcraft, were forced to chew the beans. If they vomited these up they were declared innocent but usually they died within half an hour of taking the poison. The drug caused intense thirst and as the victim's saliva increased, his stomach and respiratory tract filled with fluid, causing him to slowly drown.

The bean itself is kidney shaped and about the size of a pigeon's egg. It has a hard, shiny, chocolate coloured shell and when ground up, produces a substance similar to the "reddish-brown, snuff-like powder" mentioned in DEVI.

The experiments conducted by Thomas R. Fraser, and recorded in his paper[21] on the subject, describe the effects of both a small and large dose of the poison on one of the lower animals.

With the smaller dose, Fraser observed firstly a slight tremor, "extending from the hindquarters

---

[21] "On the Physiological Action Of The Calabar Bean" - Trans. Royal Society, Edinburgh, Vol 24, 1867.

to the forelimbs and head." This was followed by both paralysis and flaccidity of the musculature. The rectum and bladder were then emptied, the pupils contracted, the breathing became slow and irregular and a frothy mucus escaped from the mouth. After a succession of muscular contractions, death coincided with respiratory failure. The large dose caused the animal to collapse, its hind legs paralysed. After the contraction of the pupils, respiration ceased and death followed.

Sir Robert Christison's experiments,[22] were carried out in 1855 and, like many toxicologists of the period, he was himself the guinea pig. The dose he administered was short of poisonous. Twelve grains of the seed, chewed, then swallowed, acted in twenty minutes, causing giddiness and sleepiness. After emptying his stomach forcibly, he discovered that the giddiness continued. His pulse slowed down though his mental faculties remained intact, and he eventually fell into a deep sleep.

In the summer of 1864, 70 children from Liverpool ate a quantity of calabar beans which

---

[22] *ibid*

they found among the rubbish thrown out by the ship Commodore. They were treated at the Southern Hospital. One six year old, who had eaten six beans, died after severe abdominal pain, vomiting, muscular prostration, staggering gait and contracted pupils.

As the chemistry lecturer J Baker Edwards observed, after examining the body, "In criminal cases, nothing might be detected by autopsy or by chemical analysis to reveal the cause of death."[23]

The muscular paralysis the bean produces is caused by its action on the spinal cord, although it has the effect of first relaxing the musculature. It also has an unusual effect on the heart, tending to cause stoppage in the state of diastole.

The problem with the Calabar bean as a contender for the Devil's Foot is that it does not cause the hallucinations recorded by Dr Watson. It is more than possible, however, that the good doctor changed the details of the effects of the

---

[23] *Notes on the cases of Poisoning by Calabar Beans in Liverpool",
Pharm. Journal, 1864, - 65, p.99*

drug simply to dissuade the criminal fraternity from using it. Having read Edwards' notes on the subject, he would have been aware of its effects and the impossibility of pathologists proving the cause of death. Having witnessed events at Tredannack Wollas he would have trod a careful course when publicising the tragedy.[24]

---

[24] This is Verner Andersen's contention.